GROWTH & STRENGTH
~ 52 WEEKLY DEVOTIONALS ~

ADELE GROBLER

Ark House Press
PO Box 1722, Port Orchard, WA 98366 USA
PO Box 1321, Mona Vale NSW 1660 Australia
PO Box 318 334, West Harbour, Auckland 0661 New Zealand
arkhousepress.com

Cataloguing in Publication Data:
Title: Growth and Strength
ISBN: 978-0-6451080-6-4 (pbk)
Subjects: Devotional;
Other Authors/Contributors: Grobler, Adele

Design by initiateagency.com

ACKNOWLEDGEMENT

To my beautiful King Jesus, who always fights for my freedom, who always gently pushes me to greater heights, and who always cheers me on in my progress and growth in Him. This book is dedicated to You my King.

INTRODUCTION

We all go through highs and lows in life. There is not a person on this planet that has not experienced this to some degree. We love the highs! The times when things run smoothly and things work out well, but what about the lows? The times when there seems to be a cascade of things that go wrong, pain, struggles, pressures, and challenges that seem to be never ending. We would much rather not have any lows in our lives. This, however, is not something we have control over. Jesus said in John 16:33, that we will have trouble in this world but to take heart because He has already overcome the world. Challenges will come and continue to come, but we can utilise these challenges to our advantage by looking for the tools, lessons, wisdom, and knowledge that can be obtained through each challenge we face. We can then use what we have learned with the Holy Spirit's guidance, to help others that might face similar challenges. Maturity requires growth and experience. You would not entrust a toddler to be a CEO of a company. They lack the skills, knowledge, wisdom, and experience to be able to govern a company well. Instead, you entrust an experienced businessperson, who has gained the knowledge and wisdom through the years of trial and error, to help lead a company to greater success. Likewise, we move from strength to strength and growth to growth. Let us not continue to remain like infants that need to be fed spiritual milk but rather mature spiritually, being able to be fed solid food, 1 Corinthians 3:2. So, make the most out of every season, whether good or bad. Utilise it for your benefit. Ask the Holy Spirit to show you, teach you and to help you apply what you learn in your life. God does not take pleasure in our sufferings. He loves us deeply and unconditionally. He wants to see us joyful and hopeful in Him. He therefore uses what the enemy means for harm in our lives, to turn it out for good, if we would but surrender it to Him and trust Him with it all. These 52 devotionals are intended to help you grow in strength and maturity in Jesus over a one-year period. I would like to encourage you to not rush through the devotionals but rather to use them as intended. Read one devotional attentively each day during a one-week period. Take time to reflect, meditate and ponder on what is written. As you read it, ask the Holy Spirit to enlighten the eyes of your heart to greater understanding and revelation, and to help you to apply what you read and learn in your life. Doing it this way will allow for you to retain more of what you have read and learned, than if you rush through it. Take courage and know, God is for you and not against you!

TAKE TIME TO REFLECT

With You as my strength I can crush an enemy horde, advancing
through every stronghold that stands in front of me.
Psalm 18:29 (TPT)

A t the start of the year, it is always prudent to sit down and reflect upon the things God has already spoken to you about. The new strategies He has asked you to implement, the new directions He has asked you to take, things He has asked you to let go of. Have you applied what He has said? Have you done what He has asked? Have you left the things behind that He asked you to let go of? Have you started to take the next steps forward in the new directions and strategies He gave you? Taking leaps of faith? Change only occurs when we set our minds to follow. It does not happen automatically. As the Bible says, each day has its own challenges, but we do not have to face them alone. With God as our strength, we can move forward and press on towards the things He asks us to do. He equips us for where He leads. It does not matter if you feel you are equipped or not. God does not lie. If He says you can do something or asks you to do something, then that means He has already made a way for you to overcome and do it.

Declaration: I can do what my God says I can do, not because of my strength, but because of His strength.

2

LET THE HOLY SPIRIT LEAD

A man's heart plans his way, but the Lord directs his steps.
Proverbs 16:9 (NKJV)

When we are about to travel to a destination that we are not familiar with, we sit down, examine, and plan the best route we are to take to get there. We research the correct destination address and enter it into our GPS. We then feel more confident in where we are travelling to. Similarly, the Holy Spirit is our "GPS" in life. We do not know the paths or directions we are to take to get to the destination and plans God has for our lives, but He does. And the best part is, if we do take a "wrong" turn on our life journey, God is able to re-route us and bring us back on course. So, take a deep breath, trust and relax in the arms of Jesus, who loves you more than anything. Commit your decisions to Him, and the Holy Spirit will lead and guide you on the paths you are to take.

Declaration: The Holy Spirit will lead and guide me in the paths I am to take.

3

STRENGTHEN YOUR FAITH MUSCLES

For Physical training is of some value, but godliness
has value for all things, holding promise for both
the present life and the life to come.
1 Timothy 4:8 (NIV)

The Bible is like a "dumbbell" for strengthening our faith "muscles". Without it our faith cannot grow as effectively. Faith comes by hearing and hearing by the Word of God (Rom 10:17). If our inner man is full of "worldly junk" and does not receive the "exercise" and "nutrition" it requires from the Word of God, we are left feeling empty and emotionally "unhealthy". Godliness brings peace to our lives. Spend some time meditating on the Word of God and "exercising" it daily. Implement what the Bible says. You will surely reap the benefits and be glad you did!

Declaration: I "feed" daily on the Word of God. It provides me with the spiritual nutrition my soul needs.

4

GOD IS OUR FOUNDATION

He will be the sure foundation for your times, a
rich store of salvation and wisdom and knowledge;
the fear of the Lord is the key to this treasure.
Isaiah 33:6 (NIV)

The fear of the Lord is the beginning of wisdom. To fear the Lord does not mean to be scared of Him. It means to reverently be in awe and wonder of who He is and respect the fact that He is God, the Creator of everything. When we fear the Lord, we magnify who He is to us. It is in those moments that we realise our God is big, Almighty, all Powerful and on our side. He is bigger than any problem we might face. He has the wisdom and "know how" to help us endure and come out of the challenges we might face. But the key to all this is the fear of the Lord. So today, make an intentional decision to magnify Jesus higher than your circumstances and feel the weight of your troubles bow down in the Presence of the Almighty one.

Declaration: I will magnify Jesus above any circumstance I might be facing.

5

TRUST IN THE LORD

*God is not a man that He should lie, nor a son of man
that He should change His mind. Does He speak and
then not act? Does He promise and not fulfill?*
Numbers 23:19 (NIV)

God can be trusted with everything in our lives. When He gives us promises, we can be rest assured that we have what He promised us. He does not go back on His word. We are to partner with Him to take hold of those promises by faith. God's word accomplishes that which He sends it to do. There is a time for every promise to be fulfilled. Hold fast to the promises of God. Remain in faith. Though it seems to tarry, it will not tarry. He will not let you down, He won't fail you. His timing is always perfect. Keep your eyes on Him and follow where He leads.

Declaration: I can trust God fully to accomplish that which He promised me in His perfect timing.

6

YOUR PRAYERS ARE POWERFUL

Confess and acknowledge how you have offended one
another and then pray for one another to be instantly
healed, for tremendous power is released through the
passionate, heartfelt prayer of a godly believer!
James 5:16 (TPT)

There is so much power in prayer! Sometimes we become discouraged and weary of praying when we do not see our prayers immediately answered or answered in the way we would like or think. The bible tells us that the prayers of a righteous person are powerful and effective. You have been made righteous through Jesus' Blood as a believer in Christ. So, you can pray with confidence knowing that God hears your every prayer and that Jesus Himself intercedes on your behalf. So, do not lose heart! God answers our prayers according to His will and purposes. He wants us to partner with Him. There is so much strength in unity when we pray together too, for where two or more or gathered, there He is in their midst.

Declaration: As a child of God, my prayers are powerful and effective.

7

STEP BACK A LITTLE

For God is not the author of confusion, but of
peace, as in all churches of the saints.
1 Corinthians 14:33 (KJV)

Do you find yourself confused about a decision you need to make or about a certain direction you need to take? Take a step back, take a deep breath, slow down your head with all its reasoning and rationalisation. Take a moment and ask Daddy-God what you are to do or what direction you are to take. Then wait. The answer will come in His perfect timing. God does not bring confusion. He leads us in peace. Satan brings confusion, but sometimes we ourselves bring confusion to our own minds by overthinking and overanalysing things, instead of taking it to God first. Trust in the Lord with all your heart and lean not on your own understanding, in all your ways acknowledge Him and He will make your paths straight (Proverbs 3:5-6).

Declaration: When I feel confused, I take a step back, I ask God to lead me, and I then follow Him in peace.

8

BE JOYFUL IN THE LORD

Though the fig tree does not bud and there are no grapes on the
vines, though the olive crop fails and the fields produce no food,
though there are no sheep in the pen and no cattle in the stalls,
yet I will rejoice in the Lord, I will be joyful in God my Saviour.
Habakkuk 3:17-18 (NIV)

It is quite easy to praise God, be thankful and to be joyous in the Lord
when everything in our lives work out and goes well. But what about the
times when things do not go well or work out as we thought or expected?
When long awaited promises seem to take forever, when our lives are
flipped upside down and we seem to find no way of escape. How do we
respond then? Are we still thankful? Are we still praising God? Do we still
find our joy in Him during those times? God is always good. His nature
does not change. He remains faithful to us during every season of our lives,
whether it be good seasons or tough seasons. Take some time now to reflect
on the all the good things He has done for you. Rejoice in the Lord, He is
your strength.

Declaration: I am joyful in the Lord.

9

ARMOUR UP

Put on the full armour of God so that you can
take your stand against the devil's schemes.
Ephesians 6:11 (NIV)

God has given us spiritual armour to clothe ourselves with. This armour helps to protect us and to withstand the attacks of the enemy. Have you been clothing yourself with your spiritual armour? If not, I would like to encourage you to do so. Put on the helmet of salvation, taking captive wicked thoughts and wrong mindsets that the enemy tries to bombard your mind with. Then renew your mind according to the Word of God. Put on your breastplate of righteousness, making it your aim to not pursue a sinful lifestyle but aiming to live a righteous, holy and blameless life before God. Put on the belt of truth. God's Word is truth. Knowing God's nature and what the Bible says, will help you to distinguish between truth and lies. Pick up your shield of faith. When life circumstances seem to be the opposite to what God has said and spoken over your life, your shield of faith will help you to extinguish the fiery arrows of doubt from the enemy. Stand firm on God's Word and the promises He has given you. Keep believing that what God has said is true. Then, put on feet fitted with the Gospel of peace. Be ready to spread the Gospel wherever you go, making the most of every opportunity to share the great things God has done for you. Use the sword of the Spirit, which is the Word of God, by speaking out loud what the Bible and God says about your life. The sword is both a great offensive and defensive weapon against the targeted attacks from Satan.

Declaration: By putting on the full armour of God, I can withstand attacks from the enemy.

10

GROW WITH GOD

Train up a child in the way he should go, and
when he is old he will not depart from it.
Proverbs 22:6 (NKJV)

This is such an amazing bible verse for parents to hold on to. As parents, you try the best you can to help shape the choices your children will make for their good. However, everyone has free choice, and ultimately, your children will need to decide the way they will go and walk-in. But when you, as a parent, teach them God's truth and principles, and you keep praying for them you can rest assured knowing God watches over them, even when they make wrong choices in life. The same applies to our walk with Jesus. We also need to be taught and trained in God's ways, growing from "infants" being fed "milk", to mature sons and daughters of God that can be fed "solid food". God trains us and teaches us the ways we are to walk in. He does this because He loves us and knows the best for our lives. He is committed to us and wants to see us succeed. He does not want us to be harmed and therefore guides us for our safety. Ultimately, it will be our own personal choice of whether we will receive, submit, and walk in His ways and guidance.

Declaration: I embrace God's leadership and guidance in my life.

II

WALKING OUT YOUR CALLING

As a prisoner of the Lord, then, I urge you to live a
life worthy of the calling you have received.
Ephesians 4:1 (NIV)

Sometimes we can overthink the question, "what is my calling?". Our human minds like to "box" things and make it fit according to our understanding and perception. Your calling is not always rooted in a job or career. Your first calling is to be a son and daughter of God. You are a son and a daughter first. That is where your true identity lies. Walking out your calling as a son and daughter means imitating Daddy-God. And how do we imitate Him? By living a life of love - Ephesians 5:1. God is love. That is who He is. Love covers over a multitude of sins and it sums up the entire law - Galatians 5:14. Make it your aim to walk in love. Ask Jesus to soften your heart for others, to show you the "gold" He has placed inside them and to help you love them well. "By this all men will know that you are My disciples, if you love one another." – John 13:35.

Declaration: I walk in love.

12

REST IN THE LORD

*Come to Me, all you who are weary and
burdened, and I will give you rest.*
Matthew 11:28 (NIV)

Rest periods play an important part in muscle growth and regeneration. It is during these periods that the muscle fibres that were stressed during exercise begin to repair, remodel and enlarge, making them more active, resilient and stronger. The same principle applies to our walk with God. We sometimes become so distracted and bombarded with things that need to get done, that we do not always take time to rest in His presence. Resting in His presence is so important as that is where we heal spiritually. It is from this place of resting in His presence that we grow in intimacy with Him, receive emotional healing, tear down wrong mindsets, grow in our knowledge and revelation of the Lord and so forth. Make resting at Jesus' feet a priority, you will find things seem to work out better!

Declaration: I am intentional to take time daily to rest at Jesus' feet.

13

GOD LOVES TO SHARE

Call to Me and I will answer you, and will tell you
great and hidden things that you have not known.
Jeremiah 33:3 (ESV)

Daddy-God is such a loving Father. He loves to share His heart with us. He is the One with all the wisdom, knowledge, understanding, creativity, innovation, and strategies. He knows all and sees all. God wants to be part of every area of your life. He daily extends an invitation to us to come close to Him and to ask for and receive all that we need for that day. But God also likes to share and reveal things that we do not know yet. So, draw boldly to the throne of grace, and ask the Lord what He wants to share with you today. Position yourself to hear by removing any unwanted distractions. He is such an adventurous God. Ask Him to elaborate and to give you greater wisdom and understanding in what He says and reveals to you.

Declaration: I ask God daily to speak to me and share with me what is on His heart.

14

LET GO OF THE OLD, STEP INTO THE NEW

Brothers, I do not consider myself yet to have taken
hold of it. But one thing I do: Forgetting what is
behind and straining toward what is ahead.
Philippians 3:13 (NIV)

For us to move into new beginnings, we must let go of the past and move forward to what is ahead. No matter how hard you try, you cannot change the past, but you can change how you will approach your future. Living in the past will only keep you stuck and keep you from moving forward. Reminding ourselves of the past, the things that happened, the mistakes we've made, is a strategy that Satan uses to prevent us from living the abundant life Jesus died to give us. The Bible says to renew our minds. This is a deliberate choice we must make for ourselves. It does not always come easy but with God's help it can be done. Keep your focus on Jesus and where He is leading you. Soon you will find yourself moving forward in the direction He wants you to go. Surrender any old habits, old thinking patterns, and pain from the past to Jesus. Invite Him to heal your heart and help you to let go of the old. It is never too late to start! It is a New Day! Walk in it!

Declaration: I cannot change the past, but I can change the future and with Jesus' help I am making better choices!

15

CAST YOUR CARES

*And the peace of God, which transcends all understanding,
will guard your hearts and your minds in Christ Jesus.*
Philippians 4:7 (NIV)

We all face stressors and pressures of various kinds. These can come from work, relationships, finances, sickness, studying and so forth. Some things may help to reduce the impact that stress and pressures have on our bodies, such as exercising and eating healthily. It helps to balance our brain chemicals and release hormones that make us feel good about ourselves. However, the effects of exercising and eating healthily are limited. Jesus is the ultimate source of our peace. The Bible tells us to bring all our cares and anxieties to Jesus. In doing so He will exchange them for His peace. So cast all your anxiety and pressures on Him today! He can handle all of them and He wants to hear about them. Share your heart with Him about these things that trouble you. Rest in His love and His peace.

Declaration: I cast all my cares on Jesus because He cares for me.

16

YOU ARE SEEN

Higher than the highest heavens - that's how high Your
tender mercy extends! Greater than the grandeur of
heaven above is the greatness of Your loyal love, towering
over all who fear you and bow down before you!
Psalm 103:11 (TPT)

No matter where you are or where you are going, whether you are at home, travelling on holiday, or at work, God's love is right there with you. He knows exactly where you are every second of everyday. He watches over you and never takes His eyes off of you. How amazing is that! That the Creator of the universe would be so mindful of you and love you so much to keep an eye on your every step! He even knows the number of hairs on your head and when one of them falls to the ground. So, as you go about your travels and your day, remember the One who gave His life for you. You are worthy in Jesus' eyes! Seek Him, draw close to Him. Walk in the abundance of His counsel, mercy, love, and intimacy.

Declaration: No matter where I go, God sees me and loves me unconditionally.

17

BE STRONG AND COURAGEOUS

Have I not commanded you? Be strong and courageous.
Do not be frightened, and do not be dismayed, for
the Lord your God is with you wherever you go.
Joshua 1:9 (ESV)

We live in times of uncertainty. The world is rapidly changing around us, and many are fearful about the events that are happening around the world. We do not have complete control of the things that happen and will happen, but one thing is certain and remains, and that is God's unconditional love for us. God is not caught off guard and He is not taken by surprise by the events occurring in the world. He is all-knowing. He is always available to help us in our time of need. He never slumbers or sleeps. As a child of God, you do not need to fear tomorrow. For every place you step in your future, God has already been. He knows what awaits. He has already paved the way ahead of you to set you up for success and to help you come out of those difficult times. We can rest in The Father's love for us. Jesus is fighting our battles. We are not alone in the world. Be strong and courageous during your times of difficulties. Know that He is the Way Maker.

Declaration: I do not fear tomorrow for God is with me and on my side.

18

ARE YOU THANKFUL?

Enter into His gates with thanksgiving, and into His courts
with praise: be thankful unto Him, and bless His name
Psalm 100:4 (KJV)

It honours God greatly when we are thankful for the good things He does in our lives. Take some time today and do a self-reflection. How much of your prayers are focused on just supplication and requests and how much are focused on thanksgiving and praise? The Bible says to enter His gates with thanksgiving and His courts with praise. There is nothing wrong with supplications and requests, but do not forget to lift Jesus up and praise Him for all the good He has done in your life. Thankfulness helps to draw us closer to God. If you bless your child with good things and they never show a heart of gratitude towards you, how does that make you feel? But when your child is thankful and grateful for the things you do for them, does that not bless your heart? God deserves our thankfulness. He does so much for us. If you got up this morning and were able to breath, that is already something to be thankful and grateful for.

Declaration: I live a life of praise and thanksgiving; I remember all the good things Jesus has done for me.

19

GOD CARES ABOUT THE LITTLE THINGS

I lift up my eyes to the hills. From where does my help come?
My help comes from the Lord, who made heaven and earth.
Psalm 121:1-2 (ESV)

A t the start of the COVID-19 pandemic, when toilet paper was extremely limited and hard to find in stores, a family member shared something with me. They ran into a lady who seemed to have some struggles in her life, and they asked her if she needed anything such as food or toilet paper. Her response was: "No thank you, I have what I need. I just pray and ask the Holy Spirit where I need to go and buy my toilet paper from. He then tells me where I could find some and then I go to that specific store and get some." Sometimes we forget that God cares about the small things in our lives, such as our everyday need for toilet paper. We sometimes just ask for God's help with the big things, like finances, work, protection and so forth. How about today you pray and ask Him for some of the "smaller" things to bless you with. I have sometimes asked Jesus to bless me with a coffee and then He does! His heart towards us is full of love and kindness. Sometimes we have not because we ask not.

Declaration: God cares about the big and small things in my life.

20

TAKE IT STEP BY STEP

Behold, I will do a new thing, now it shall spring
forth; shall you not know it? I will even make a
road in the wilderness and rivers in the desert.
Isaiah 43:19 (NKJV)

God is the God of new beginnings! If you have felt like a failure in life and hoped for a new start, look no further! God's incredible love and mercy can change you in ways you could never even imagine! New beginnings do not necessarily mean a change in our physical circumstances. Allowing God to change our hearts and perspectives in how we view circumstances and situations, is what truly brings major changes in our lives. We reap benefits such as greater joy, freedom, and peace in our hearts when we fully surrender to His ways. We must partner with Him if we want to see these changes happening. We cannot do it in our own strength. Talk with Jesus about it and follow His instructions. In the end, you will not regret it! Just take it step by step, day by day, and you will get there. Do not look at mistakes as failing. Change your perspective and understand that mistakes help to teach you a better way. God does not see you as a failure. He will help you in your weakness. He is the one who can make your crooked places straight.

Declaration: It is not too late for me; I can have a fresh start with God's help.

21

LET GO OF OFFENCE

Do not pay attention to every word people say, or you
may hear your servant cursing you - for you know in your
heart that many times you yourself have cursed others.
Ecclesiastes 7:21-22 (NIV)

Offence is a weapon the enemy uses to bring separation in relationships. Offence can come in various forms such as misunderstandings and misinterpretation of what people say. There are also less subtle ways, such as hearing gossip about ourselves that is not true or accurate. The Bible tells us not to pay attention to every word people say about us, as it might not always be something good, and it reminds us that there have been times when we ourselves have spoken ill of others. We all have, in some shape or form, said something in the past that might have misrepresented someone and caused offence. We all fall short. Forgiving offences is not necessarily for the benefit of the person who caused the offence, but rather for you. When you do not forgive offences, it leaves an open door to the enemy. So, keep that door shut and your heart free. Forgive the offences of others, keeping in mind that God has forgiven yours when you asked Him to.

Declaration: I am quick to forgive offences

22

USE YOUR DOUBLE-EDGED SWORD

Let the high praises of God be in their mouth,
and a two-edge sword in their hand.
Psalm 149:6 (NKJV)

Praising God is so powerful! Psalm 24:7 (NKJV) says: "Lift up your heads, O you gates! And be lifted up, you everlasting doors! And the King of Glory shall come in." When we praise and worship God, our focus is purely on Him and not our circumstances. Whatever we focus on, we magnify. You do not have to have it all together to be able to praise Him. Just come as you are. Praise and worship bring us into a deeper place of intimacy with Jesus. It is from a lifestyle of praise and worship that we grow more, hear more, and enjoy Him more. There is something incredibly special in worshipping Jesus in various forms. From singing, dancing, kneeling, prostrating ourselves in humility, playing musical instruments, speaking poetry and so forth. Worship can also be done in our hearts, making a melody to the Lord as we go about our day. Praising and worshiping the Lord also defeats the enemy. It is like a two-edge sword in our hands. Nothing confuses the enemy more than praising Jesus when things go pear-shaped. So, fight back! When you feel defeated by life's circumstances take some time and just praise the Lord for who and what He is and see the change it brings in your life!

Declaration: Praise and worship helps defeat the enemy

23

23

WHAT IS IN YOUR HEART?

The good man brings good things out of the good
stored up in his heart, and the evil man brings evil
things out of the evil stored up in his heart. For out
of the overflow of his heart his mouth speaks.

Luke 6:45 (NIV)

What is going on in your heart? Is it full of anger, bitterness, resentment, offence, unforgiveness, greed, lust, envy, jealousy and so forth? No matter how hard we try to hide what goes on in our hearts, eventually it will come out of our mouths and reveal what has been hidden in our hearts. As the Bible says, a good tree cannot produce bad fruit, neither can a bad tree bear good fruit. We are recognised by our fruit. This is not to make us feel condemned but rather to reflect and see where the deep-rooted issues in our hearts come from, and to take that before Jesus and ask Him to help us to get rid of it so that we can bear good fruit for Him.

Declaration: I aim at working with the Lord to get rid of the "bad" fruit in my heart so that I can bloom and burst forth with good fruit for Him.

24

HOLD YOUR TONGUE

Whoever of you loves life and desires to see many good days,
keep your tongue from evil and your lips from speaking lies.
Turn from evil and do good; seek peace and pursue it.
Psalm 34:12-14 (NIV)

Our mouths can get us into a lot of trouble. In James chapter 3, it talks about the tongue being a fire, a world of iniquity. It only takes a simple word to hurt someone's feelings, to betray a confidence, to bring suspicion about another person and so forth. We all fall short in this. There is no man on earth that is always perfect in what he says or does. However, if we would like to see many good days, we are to keep our tongues from evil and our lips from speaking lies – 1 Peter 3:10. The power of life and death lies in the tongue – Proverbs 18:21. If you speak death over yourself, others and circumstances, you will reap destruction. However, if you speak life, you will reap blessings and a sure reward. Let us make our minds up to keep watch over our mouths, to think before we speak. Let us use our mouths to build each other up, to bring healing, to inspire, to encourage. Ask the Holy Spirit to help you guard your mouth and choose your words wisely. We will all need to give an account to God for every careless word we speak – Matthew 12:36.

Declaration: I work with the Holy Spirit to watch what I say, to speak life and not death in every circumstance.

25

BE KIND AND COMPASSIONATE

*Be completely humble and gentle; be patient, bearing
with one another in love. Make every effort to keep
the unity of the Spirit through the bond of peace.*
Ephesians 4:2-3 (NIV)

We all face trials of various kinds. We all want to do the best we can and be the best person we can be. We are all in the process of growth and renewal. We all make mistakes, we all fall short, we all say and do things that we should not. Every person that you meet is facing a battle that you know nothing about. When we ourselves are going through difficulties, we sometimes forget that others might be too. So be kind and compassionate to every person that you encounter. Guard your heart as to not take offence. You do not know what challenges another person might be facing, just as they do not know what you are facing. Do your best to keep the peace. Love your enemies and do good to those who come against you. You are only accountable for your actions and responses, not theirs.

Declaration: I will be kind and compassionate to every person I encounter, aiming to keep peace wherever I go.

26

YOU DO NOT NEED TO FIGHT FOR GOD'S LOVE

This is love: He loved us long before we loved Him. It was
His love, not ours. He proved it by sending His Son to be
the pleasing sacrificial offering to take away our sins.
1 John 4:10 (TPT)

God loves you unconditionally. Jesus died for your sins while you were yet a sinner, not when you already had it all together and did everything perfectly. We can never do anything to earn God's love. It is by His love that He created each one of us uniquely for Him, so that we could walk with Him daily and have an intimate relationship with Him. He is not a God far off, but a God that is near. No number of "good" deeds you do can earn that kind of love. It is because of His love for us, that we fall in love with Him. Jesus died and rose again to cloth you with His righteousness so that you can come close to Daddy-God. It is from that knowledge of His love for us, that we want to grow and live godly lives before Him. When you love someone, you want to do those things that you know will please them, not for their acceptance or approval, but out of love. Draw close to Him and rest in His Divine love for you.

Declaration: God loves me unconditionally, simply for being me.

27

LET JESUS SOFTEN YOUR HEART

I will give you a new heart and put a new spirit in you; I will
remove from you your heart of stone and give you a heart of flesh.
Ezekiel 36:26 (NIV)

As we journey through life, our hearts sometimes become hardened by
the difficulties, trials, and sufferings we face. We then tend to be less
compassionate and empathetic towards the sufferings of others. Our love
seems to grow a bit cold, and we seem to have less patience with those
around us. Outbursts of anger and frustration seem to follow. Thankfully,
we do not have to stay that way. When we surrender the things that harden
our hearts to Jesus, asking Him to take care of it, to bring healing and
remove our hearts of stone. He is faithful, and He does. He will constantly
help us to have a heart of flesh instead of a heart of stone when we continue
to lean into Him and work with Him, following in obedience.

Declaration: I guard and examine my heart as to not allow for it to become
a heart of stone.

28

ARE YOU JEALOUS?

What causes fights and quarrels among you? Don't they
come from your desires that battle within you? You want
something but don't get it. You kill and covet, but you
cannot have what you want. You quarrel and fight. You
do not have, because you do not ask God. When you ask,
you do not receive, because you ask with wrong motives,
that you may spend what you get on your pleasures.

James 4:1-3 (NIV)

A jealous heart reflects discontentment with circumstances. When you want or desire something so much that it consumes your thoughts, your heart and even your actions, it creates an open door for Satan to torment you with those very same desires. The Bible teaches us to keep our minds fixed on the things above and not on the earthly things. This does not mean that it is wrong to want or desire something, but sometimes it can become an idol if it is all we think about and want to pursue. Even the promises God gives us can sometimes become an idol when we do not see it come to pass when we want to. Our desires for it can become so intense, that we become discontented and then start complaining that we have not received it yet. Discontentment, jealousy, envy and complaining does not please God. Seek God's heart and not His hand. Be grateful and content with what you have. Seek God's Righteousness and His kingdom first and all these things will be given to you besides – Matthew 6:33. When we put God first in our hearts and minds, our motives then tend to align with Kingdom rather than the flesh. Examine your motives. What is the root behind your desires?

Declaration: I seek God and His Kingdom first

29

THE BIBLE IS OUR MANUAL FOR LIFE

All Scripture is breathed out by God and profitable for teaching,
for reproof, for correction, and for training in righteousness, that
the man of God may be complete, equipped for every good work.
2 Timothy 3:16-17 (ESV)

The Word of God is living and active, sharper than any double-edged
sword, it tests the thoughts and attitudes of our hearts - Hebrews 4:12.
The Bible is God's living Word that He has given us to help teach us how to
live while here on this earth. The Bible teaches us about God's nature, His
love for us, as well as who we are in Christ. Reading and applying what the
Bible says, should be a priority in our lives. Not doing it out of a "must do",
ticking off a list, but rather approaching it in humility out of a "want to",
having a heart hungry to hear what God wants to say and teach us daily. As
you read and "study" the Bible, ask the Holy Spirit to enlighten the eyes of
your heart to better understanding and revelation of what has been written,
and ask Him to help you apply it in your life.

Declaration: I meditate and study on the Word of God daily.

30

GOD FIGHTS FOR YOU

The Lord will fight for you; you need only to be still.
Exodus 14:14 (NIV)

As you go about your day, remember that God is with you wherever you go and wherever you step. Every battle that you might face and that may come your way, know that you are not facing it alone. Jesus is right there with you, ready to help you, ready to fight your battles on your behalf. Surrender the battle over to Him. Ask Him to lead and guide you as to what you should do in the battle, how to approach it, how to act and respond to it. Battles differ, and so does the strategies to overcome them. We need to rely on God's wisdom as to the approaches and strategies rather than relying on our own insights. Trust that as you commit your way to the Lord, He will make your paths straight and direct your steps. Ask Daddy-God to send His angels to help you and engage in the battle with you. Remember, you are fighting from victory, not for victory. Through Christ we are more than conquerors.

Declaration: I am not alone in my battles; God fights for me.

31

DO NOT FEAR SUDDEN DISASTER

Have no fear of sudden disaster or of the ruin that
overtakes the wicked, for the Lord will be your confidence
and will keep your foot from being snared.
Proverbs 3:25-26 (NIV)

God is Sovereign above all. He is greater than natural disasters, war, viruses etc. As a child of God you can rest in the confidence of knowing that Daddy-God loves you more than anything. The Bible says to not fear sudden disaster or the ruin that over takes the wicked. It does not mean that you won't have to face tough times and situations, it means that no matter what you face, it won't separate you from God's love for you. If you have given your life to Christ and are walking with Him, you need not fear the life to come either. For when your life here on earth is finished, you get to spend eternity in His loving presence. So take heart in whatever circumstance you might find yourself in today. Know that God is for you and not against you.

Declaration: I don't fear tomorrow, the Lord is my confidence and He will keep me.

32

RUN YOUR RACE WELL

Do you not know that in a race all the runners run, but only
one gets the prize? Run in such a way as to get the prize.

1 Corinthians 9:24 (NIV)

We only get to live once on this earth. How will you run your race? This world and everything in it are passing away, what will you have left at the end of the day? Do you make time to build and work on your relationship with Jesus, or do you keep putting Him at the back burner saying, "I will pray and read my bible later as I have other things to take care of"? What can be more valuable than getting to know the Almighty God and making time for Him and doing life with Him. If you make Jesus a priority in your life, you will find that somehow you are able to accomplish more in a day than if you do not. Seek Him early, receive your strength from Him and rely on Him to help you in all your responsibilities.

Declaration: I make spending time with Jesus a priority in my life.

33

RECEIVE GOD'S LOVING CORRECTION

*If you readily receive correction, you are walking on the path
to life. But if you reject rebuke, you're guaranteed to go astray.*
Proverbs 10:17 (TPT)

Out of His great love for us, God will sometimes bring us correction. Receiving correction or rebukes are not always pleasant. It is not something that tends to excite us and it "hurts" a little, as it calls for our flesh to die a little more and our spirit man to grow stronger in Him. Whenever the Lord sends His rebukes or corrections, it is always for our benefit. It helps to bring us back in alignment with Him and protects us from wrong choices and decisions that can bring grief to us later. So, rejoice when the Lord corrects you, because that means you are His child and He cares for you and cares about the ways you take. Apply His corrections in your life and you will grow wiser on your life's journey.

Declaration: I gladly receive the Lord's corrections and rebukes in my life

34

RENEW YOUR STRENGTH

But those who hope in the Lord will renew their strength.
They will soar on wings like eagles; they will run and
not grow weary, they will walk and not be faint.
Isaiah 40:31 (NIV)

Do you feel tired, weary, or drained? Are you trying to regain your strength on your own? Is it working? We do have a responsibility to do all we can to combat our weariness through sleeping enough, eating healthily, exercising, relaxing and resting. But we sometimes forget the most important part, which is to rest in His presence to regain our strength. Ask the Holy Spirit to fill you with His strength and power, to comfort you, to encourage you and to renew His hope in your heart. The Bible says to ask and receive, and we do not always receive because we do not always ask. So, ask Him for renewed strength to soar like an eagle on the currents of life. You will be surprised how He will empower you through His grace to do and accomplish all that is needed in that day.

Declaration: When I need strength, I rest in God and am empowered to do all I need to do.

35

PRAY FOR YOUR CITY

*Also, seek the peace and prosperity of the city to
which I have carried you into exile. Pray to the Lord
for it, because if it prospers, you too will prosper.*
Jeremiah 29:7 (NIV)

We all want peace and prosperity, especially in the cities and nations we reside in. Are you praying for your city and your nation? Are you praying for your neighbourhood, the church you go to, the schools your children attend, your workplace? If you are not, I want to encourage you to do so. There is so much power in prayer when we partner with God to see transformation in our cities, nations and places that effect our daily lives. The enemy is constantly trying to take and claim these territories. When we, as children of God, sit back and become complacent, things start to go very wrong. God calls us to take dominion and rule. So do not allow the enemy to gain ground over your territory. Fight the good fight of faith, stand in your authority in Christ and pray for light to break through the darkness in these places.

Declaration: I pray for the prosperity and peace for my city and my nation and I decree all darkness to flee in Jesus' Name.

36

GOD TURNS THINGS AROUND FOR OUR GOOD

You intended to harm me, but God intended it for good to
accomplish what is now being done, the saving of many lives.
Genesis 50:20 (NIV)

God is the God of the impossible. He can work every bad situation out for good. Just like Joseph in the Bible, where his brothers meant to harm him, God's Sovereign protection was still over Joseph, and his life was spared. Joseph had to go through many hardships and unjust circumstances, but he continued walking with God. He trusted God and God worked out everything for his good in the end. Likewise, we do not have control over the actions of others or circumstances we must face, but if we continually submit it to God and keep following Him and walking in His ways, He will work things together for the good of those who love Him.

Declaration: God is my Vindicator, and He can use the good and the bad in my life to bring Him glory and honour.

37

LET YOUR LIGHT SHINE

Let your light so shine before men, that they may see your
good works and glorify your Father which is in heaven.
Matthew 5:16 (KJV)

When you observe a lighthouse at night, you see the rotating beam of light stretching to the furthest ends. It is amazing how such a simple light can make such a difference in the darkness, informing ships that they are close to land, bringing them hope for harbouring and aiding navigation, or warning the ships that they are approaching dangerous areas. Likewise, we are carriers of hope in this life. There are times when darkness seems to be all around us. We, as children of God, carry His Holy Spirit on the inside of us, sparkling and shining just like the lighthouse, displaying His hope to those who seem to be "lost at sea" and wandering in darkness. We "light" up the sky for them, pointing them to Jesus, the Author and Finisher of our faith. Do not be afraid or ashamed of His light on the inside of you. It can truly make all the difference to someone else's life. Let your light shine brightly!

Declaration: God's Glory shines through me

38

GUARD YOUR WAYS

The highway of the upright avoids evil; he
who guards his way guards his life.
Proverbs 16:17 (NIV)

There are many benefits we reap when we aim to live righteous and upright lives before God. One of the main benefits is a clean conscience. A clean conscience produces peace in our lives. When we choose to live deceitfully, gossiping about others, lusting, stealing, practicing habitual sins and pleasures, there is an "unrest" or "nervousness" we feel in our conscience. We do not want those things to be revealed and be found out by others. Hence, we try and compensate by trying to cover things up. The Bible says that there is nothing hidden that will not be revealed. So even if we try and "cover" these things up, a time will come that it will be exposed. Repent and partner with God to change. Avoid evil and guard your choices. Choose to make good and right choices instead of deliberately sinful ones. Make God a priority in your life. You will reap the benefits of peace and rest in your heart.

Declaration: I choose to do what is right.

39

KEEP YOUR COMMITMENTS

Simply let your 'yes' be 'yes' and your 'no', 'no';
anything beyond this comes from the evil one.
Matthew 5:37 (NIV)

Honesty and integrity are, sadly, hard to come by these days. People say one thing, and then do another. People change their minds based on their feelings and there is not a lot of follow through on their words. This is not to be so. The Bible says let your 'yes' be 'yes and your 'no', be 'no', otherwise we give foothold to the enemy. A double minded man is unstable in all he does, he is like a wave of the sea being tossed backwards and forwards. It is important to keep our commitments. We can sometimes miss out on some great blessings and opportunities to advance the Kingdom of God if we easily change our minds. Be a dependable person that can be relied upon and stick to your commitments. Do not make any commitments in haste and when your emotions are at a heightened level. First, pray about it, evaluate, and consider if you would be able to follow through on that commitment, and then decide.

Declaration: I am not a double minded person, but I let my 'yes' be 'yes' and my 'no', be 'no'.

40

RECEIVE GOD'S MERCY

The steadfast love of the Lord never ceases; His
mercies never come to an end; they are new
every morning; great is Your faithfulness.
Lamentations 3:22-23 (ESV)

God is so good and merciful to us. He is faithful throughout the ages. He never gives up on us. No matter how badly we have messed up, Jesus' arms are open wide to receive us. By His blood we are cleansed of all our sins and unrighteousness. He already paid the price for us. All we need to do is receive His forgiveness, His mercy, grace, and love and walk boldly in the knowledge that He will remain faithful to us no matter what, for He cannot disown Himself. Every day is a fresh start with Him. Make it your aim to repent of any sins and to follow Him in obedience each day. We go from strength to strength, growth to growth, glory to glory, grace to grace. Never give up. Keep moving forward. He will help you get your act together, just invite Him to lead, guide and do what needs to be done in your life. He is the potter and you the clay.

Declaration: I receive God's mercy and forgiveness each day.

41

DO NOT LIVE TO PLEASE MAN

There's trouble ahead when you live for the approval of others, saying what flatters them, doing what indulges them. Popularity contests are not truth contests – look how many scoundrel preachers were approved by your ancestors! Your task is to be true, not popular.

Luke 6:26 (MSG)

The Bible says that the fear of man will prove to be a snare. When we fear man more than God, we open ourselves up to peer pressure. We then tend to compromise on our beliefs and values and are then more likely to do things that are not pleasing to God or in alignment with His Word. This in turn opens doors to the enemy, allowing him access to ensnare us and bring destruction in our lives. God created you to be who you are. You are unique and one of a kind. If you need to compromise who you are to please people, then they are most likely not the right people for you. The right people will love you and respect you for who you are. Never value what people say about you more than what God says about you. What God says about you is truth and can always be trusted. Find your worth, value and identity in Jesus.

Declaration: I fear God more than man.

42

DO NOT BE DISCOURAGED

And don't allow yourselves to be weary or disheartened
in planting good seeds, for the season of reaping the
wonderful harvest you've planted is coming!
Galatians 6:9 (TPT)

When we do our best to do the right thing, and we do not see the results we want to see, we tend to become discouraged and are more likely to then give up on the situation or person. For example, if you work for a boss who is not easy to get along with, out of your respect for God, you will do your best to treat them the right way and to pray for them. But as time passes, you may discern no change in their behaviour towards you, even though you try your best to be friendly and compliant. The Bible says to not become weary in doing good. At the proper time you will reap a harvest from your well doing if you do not give up. God sees everything. It honours Him when you do the right thing even when it hurts. He will reward you in His perfect timing. So never give up on doing good. Ask Jesus to be your strength when you are feeling weak. You can do all things with His help.

Declaration: I continue to do good; it honours God.

43

KEEP YOUR FOCUS ON JESUS

You will keep him in perfect peace, whose mind
is stayed on You, because he trusts in You.
Isaiah 26:3 (NKJV)

Are you feeling discouraged, anxious, or even frustrated? If you are, then ask yourself this: "What am I thinking about? Where is my focus? Am I thinking about a situation I have no control over, trying to figure it out? Is my mind and focus on Jesus or other things? It helps to take some time and reflect on what is going on in your thoughts. When we make it our priority to focus on Jesus and constantly surrender situations over to Him, exchanging it for His peace, we in turn become more peaceful. Practice the art of surrendering and letting go. There is something so powerful in resting in the knowledge that God's got you. He knows what to do in every situation and knows what you need before you even ask Him. Nothing is out of His reach. So, take a deep breath. Give Him your discouragement, anxiety and frustrations and thankfully receive His peace.

Declaration: I keep my focus on Jesus as I know I can trust Him with everything in my life

44

YOU CANNOT HIDE FROM THE HOLY SPIRIT

Where can I go from Your Spirit? Where can I flee from Your
Presence? If I go up to the heavens, You are there; if I make
my bed in the depths, You are there. If I rise on the wings of
the dawn, if I settle on the far side of the sea, even there Your
hand will guide me, Your right hand will hold me fast.
Psalm 139:7-10 (NIV)

There is no place on earth where you can go where God does not see you
and is able to reach you. No matter how much we might mess up in life,
the countless mistakes we make, God comes to where we are, even in our
messes, to help us get out of the 'holes' we dig or find ourselves in. Your life
can never be too messed up, you can never be too far gone. God's grace for
you is overwhelming. His deepest desire is for you to walk in freedom from
the things that entangle and hold you down. So, if you feel like a mess today,
just remember, even Jesus' disciples did not always have it all together. Look at
Peter, he denied Jesus three times. Thomas doubted that Jesus was raised from
the dead. John and James asked Jesus if they should call for fire from heaven
to burn the people who did not welcome Him. Jesus died and was raised again
for your sins, not for your perfection. So, do not run and hide from Him, but
run towards Him. He is the only One who can truly help you start fresh.

Declaration: I am not too far gone for God to reach me; I just have to turn
to Him.

45

ARE YOU BUSY?

What does man gain from all his labour
at which he toils under the sun?
Ecclesiastes 1:3 (NIV)

Everyone is busy. Busy with work, busy with studies, busy with family, busy with other activities. It has become such a natural part of life to be "busy". Have you asked yourself lately "what is the fruit and result from all my busyness?", "what do I have to show for it at the end of the day?", "am I keeping busy with things that will have eternal value?". If you are feeling the strain and strife in your life from being busy, perhaps you need to take some time and sit with Jesus and ask Him about your schedule. Ask Him if what you are currently doing is His best for your life. Are your days filled with "good" things or "God things"? What things are you to remove and what things are you to add to your schedule. He knows you and your life better than you. God wants to be involved in every area of our lives, including our schedules. Do not rely on your own wisdom or insight but ask Him for guidance.

Declaration: I don't rely on myself to create my schedule, but I rely on God to help me prioritise.

46

ARE YOU PRIDEFUL?

"Has not My hand made all these things, and so they came into
being?" declares the Lord. "This is the one I esteem: he who
is humble and contrite in spirit, and trembles at My word."
Isaiah 66:2 (NIV)

In 1 Peter 5:5, it says that God resists the proud but He gives grace to
the humble. God hates pride. Do you have pride in your heart? Do you
set yourself above God? Do you boast in all your achievements without
acknowledging the One who enabled you to achieve these things in the
first place? Are you selfish? Are you self-absorbed? Do you question God
in a disrespectful manner? Do you murmur and complain against Him
when things do not go your own way? Do you boast about who you know
and who your friends are, more than boasting about Jesus? These are some
questions to help you examine your heart for pride. Sometimes we are not
"promoted" in the promises God gave us, because our hearts are not ready
to handle it. Ask the Lord to show you if you are harbouring pride, and
then to help you remove it from your life. Walk humbly with God and in
due season He will lift you up.

Declaration: I humble myself before the Lord.

47

BE SHARPENED

If the iron is blunt, and one does not sharpen the edge, he
must use more strength, but wisdom helps one to succeed.
Ecclesiastes 10:10 (ESV)

A re you investing time to sharpen your relationship with Jesus? Do you
sit with Him, allowing Him to remove the "bluntness" out of your life,
and to polish you? Like an axe that becomes blunt over time from being
put to work, likewise, we can become spiritually "blunt" if we do not take
time to be sharpened and polished by Him. Ask the Holy Spirit to reveal
the areas in your life that need "sharpening". Whether it is to be more compassionate, patient, gentle, loving or perhaps to say no to certain hobbies
and pleasures that do not please Him. Whatever it is that is keeping you
"blunt" spiritually, He is the One who can reveal and help sharpen those
areas in your life.

Declaration: I keep my relationship with Jesus a priority and do not allow
myself to become spiritually blunt.

48

STOP BEATING YOURSELF UP

But He said to me, "My grace is sufficient for you, for My power is
made perfect in weakness." Therefore I will boast all the more gladly
about my weaknesses, so that Christ's power may rest on me.

2 Corinthians 12:9 (NIV)

Do you beat yourself up every time you make a mistake, every time you fall
short, every time you seem to not get things done the "right" way, or how
others would do it? Well, the great news is, that God's grace is sufficient for
you. You do not need to rely on yourself to do things well. You can rely on
His strength, wisdom, and power to do what you need to do, and even if you
do not do it perfectly, His grace is there to cover you. You are not going to be
a perfect human, no matter how hard you try. There is no point in beating
yourself up. It just wastes precious time and energy. All you can do is the best
you can with what you have, and to be willing to learn from your mistakes
and to be open to grow and work with the Holy Spirit each day. God loves
you for you. He is aware of your weaknesses as a human and wants to help
you with them. God has already equipped you to do what you need to do.
Just bring your "two fish" and "five loathes" and watch Him multiply it.

Declaration: I do not beat myself up every time I fall short, but I receive
God's grace in my weakness.

49

PONDER ON GOD'S GLORIOUS WORKS

How great are your works, O Lord, how profound your thoughts!
Psalm 92:5 (NIV)

When your mind tries to play tricks on you, and you start to feel overwhelmed about the uncertain times we are living in, remember this: we serve an excessively big God! Make yourself a cup of coffee or tea, sit down, take a deep breath, then look around you. Look at all of creation. The butterflies, the grass, the trees, the clouds, the sun, the mountains, all of it. Remember that God created all these things just by simply speaking it into being. Our human minds cannot comprehend the vastness of His Almighty power. And yet, of everything He created, He created you. And of everything He could love, He loves you. Of everything in creation that He cares for, He cares for you. So, lift up your eyes to the heavens. Consider the works of His hands and rest in the peaceful assurance that the God of the universe is holding you in the palm of His hand, and nobody can snatch you out of it!

Declaration: When I feel overwhelmed, I take some time and reflect on how big my God is.

50

DOES YOUR FAITH SHOW?

In the same way, faith by itself, if it is not
accompanied by action, is dead.
James 2:17 (NIV)

We all have faith in something. For example, you may have faith that your alarm clock will wake you up in the morning so you can be on time for work. You may have faith that your car will start so you are able to drive to work. But what about your faith in God? We sometimes use the term "faith" so casually, saying "oh, I have faith in God", but my question to you is, to what degree is your faith?

Can your faith be seen? For example, if you say you have faith that God will help you to secure a job, do you then become frightened and shy away from a job opportunity He brings your way because you think you are not good enough or have what it takes because it requires more than your current skill level? Or do you accept the job in faith because you know that God has provided the opportunity for you and so He will help you do what is needed? Let your faith be seen in your life choices.

Declaration: I step out in faith for God is with Me.

51

BE READY FOR SERVICE

Be dressed ready for service and keep your lamps burning, like men
waiting for their master to return from a wedding banquet, so that when
he comes and knocks they can immediately open the door for him.
Luke 12:35-36 (NIV)

Every day is an opportunity to extend God's Kingdom here on the earth.
It is such a blessing knowing that God wants to work in and through
each one of us to accomplish His will here on earth. The question is, do we
allow ourselves to be interruptible by the Holy Spirit as we go about our
day? Are we willing to stop and help the one He asks us to help, or do we
"close" our ears and keep doing what we want to instead? God always has
a good reason for stopping us during our day to be Jesus' hands and feet
for others. Sometimes we are unaware of Him wanting to work through
us in a particular situation. The good news is, you can become more and
more discerning and aware of His Presence by investing time, in the secret
place, with Him. Spending time talking with Him, reading, and studying
the Bible, worshipping Him and stepping out when He asks you in order
to gain experience with Him, are some ways to grow in discernment. Make
yourself more available to be used by God and see what happens!

Declaration: I remain attentive and sensitive to the Holy Spirit's
promptings.

52

RECEIVE FORGIVENESS

*If we confess our sins, He is faithful and just and will forgive
us our sins and purify us from all unrighteousness.*
1 John 1:9 (NIV)

Jesus paid a high price for our sins. God knew that when sin entered the world through the disobedience of Adam and Eve, that no matter how hard we tried, we would not be able to do everything right. That is why Daddy-God already had in mind to send Jesus to die for our sins and to be raised again, so that through believing in Jesus, we would be victorious over sin with His help. God is not unjust. He is aware of our weaknesses and failures. He wants us to draw closer to Him, repent of our sins and receive His forgiveness and help us to grow in Him to live holy and Godly lives. So, have confidence in approaching God. His love is so deep for you, that even when you have sinned, He wants you to receive His forgiveness and grow in a deeper relationship with Him. Do not forget to forgive yourself either. Sometimes we are wiling to receive God's forgiveness, the forgiveness of others, but not ourselves. If you have been living in unforgiveness towards yourself, now is the time to let go and move forward.

Declaration: I am forgiven.

www.ingramcontent.com/pod-product-compliance
Lightning Source LLC
LaVergne TN
LVHW021624080426
835510LV00019B/2751